OH, HOW WE NEED
Each Other

A MESSAGE FOR WOMEN

SHERI DEW

DESERET
BOOK

SALT LAKE CITY, UTAH

Text for this booklet was adapted from *The Beginning of Better Days: Divine Instruction to Women from the Prophet Joseph Smith* (Salt Lake City: Deseret Book, 2012).

Book design: © Deseret Book
Art direction: Richard Erickson
Design: Sheryl Dickert Smith
Design motifs from Shutterstock © krishnasomya and biddy.

ISBN 978-1-62972-426-3

Printed in the United States of America
Sun Print Solutions, Salt Lake City, UT

10 9 8 7 6 5 4 3 2 1

Relief Society and the Prophet Joseph Smith

If I were identifying major themes in my life, one of them would have to be Relief Society, though when I was called in my early twenties to serve as the Relief Society president of a young adult ward, I was flabbergasted. Nothing about me matched my image of a Relief Society leader. "I don't bake bread, I can't quilt, I love sports," I stammered, listing everything that would surely disqualify me. But the bishop said the Lord had spoken, and that was that.

Attending to the varied and often emotionally charged needs of more than two hundred young-adult-age women trying to find themselves was eye-opening, around-the-clock work—and particularly for someone who was having her first serious leadership experience. But it gave me a front-row seat from which to watch the Lord work miracle after miracle in the lives of His daughters. It was at that young age that I began to experience the power of a woman's faith. And it was when I began to see that there was a lot more to Relief Society than met the eye.

Fast-forward a decade. My thirties were filled with lots of Church service but also escalating frustration. I had kept a stiff upper lip about not yet marrying, but by thirty-five, I'd lost my sense of humor about everyone (all of my siblings, most of my friends) getting married except me and had become deeply discouraged about it all. In addition to my longing for a companion, the window on my bearing children was narrowing, and the fear that I might never have children was closing its icy grip around me. I spent a lot of time on my knees and in the temple pleading for a family of my own. I couldn't understand why I was being denied such a righteous desire, nor could I sustain a feeling of peace.

Ironically, it was then that I was called to serve as the Relief Society president in a stake comprised almost entirely of young families—in other words, a stake filled with women living the life I wanted. Because my life was different from theirs, I quickly realized that I would have to be the one to build a bridge between my singleness and their lives filled with family. I prayed a lot, combed the scriptures, and practically took up residence in the temple seeking guidance on how to serve, relate to, and provide leadership for the sisters in my stake.

One day when I felt stymied about a message I was to deliver at a stake women's conference, I started looking through materials I'd collected while serving a few years earlier as a member of the Relief Society general board under President Barbara Winder. There, buried in a file, was my copy of the *Minutes of the Female Relief Society of Nauvoo* (hereafter *Minutes*). I had studied them while serving on the general board, quoted from them, and then filed them away when I'd been released.

But on that day, the *Minutes* that Eliza R. Snow had recorded of the first Relief Society meetings and later packed across the plains reached through a century and a half and spoke to me. I began to read, underline, and scrawl notes in the margins. In particular, I was captivated by the centerpieces of those *Minutes*— six sermons the Prophet Joseph Smith delivered to the sisters between March and August of 1842.

I had read these documents before—I had even quoted from them—but somehow it had never lodged in my mind that we had a record of sermons Joseph Smith had delivered specifically to women.

At this point, let me ask the obvious: Does what the Prophet Joseph taught a relatively small group of Latter-day Saint women more than 175 years ago matter now?

I believe his teachings and counsel to women have never mattered more.

Joseph Smith is the Prophet entrusted with ushering in this final dispensation—the man John Taylor said did more "save Jesus only, for the salvation of men in this world, than any other man."[1] Joseph not only saw the Father and the Son but was, as President George Q. Cannon explained, "visited constantly by angels. . . . He had vision after vision in order that his mind might be fully saturated with a knowledge of the things of God."[2] This is the man who declared that if you could "gaze into heaven five minutes, you would know more than you would by reading all that ever was written on the subject."[3] It is the man who on another occasion said of one vision in particular, "I could explain

3

a hundred fold more than I ever have of the glories of the kingdoms manifested to me in the vision, were I permitted, and were the people prepared to receive them."[4]

Do you and I want to know what the Prophet of the Restoration—the Prophet tutored constantly by heavenly messengers—taught the women of Nauvoo and thus all women of this dispensation? Surely the answer is a resounding yes!

May I suggest that there is a second reason the Prophet's sermons have meaning for us today. President Joseph F. Smith declared that the Relief Society holds a unique place in the Lord's Church: "This is . . . the oldest auxiliary organization of the Church and it is of the first importance. It has not only to deal with the necessities of the poor, the sick and the needy, but a part of its duty—and the larger part, too—is to look after the spiritual welfare and salvation of the mothers and daughters of Zion; to see that none is neglected, but that all are guarded against misfortune, calamity, the powers of darkness, and the evils that threaten them in the world. It is the duty of the Relief Societies to look after the spiritual welfare of themselves and of all the female members of the Church."[5]

President Joseph F. Smith returned to this theme again, stating: "[The Relief Society] is divinely made, divinely authorized, divine instituted, divinely ordained of God to minister for the salvation of souls of women and of men. Therefore there is not any organization that can compare with it, . . . that can ever occupy the same stand and platform that this can. . . . Make [Relief Society] first, make it foremost, make it the highest, the best and the deepest of any organization in existence in the world. You are called by the voice of the Prophet of God to do it, to be uppermost, to be the greatest and the best, the purest and the most devoted to the right."[6]

From the outset, the Prophet Joseph clearly signaled the Relief Society's vital commission in building faith and testimony among latter-day women and their families and in providing a way for sisters to let their light shine. The subjects he covered in his sermons to the sisters of Nauvoo reflect a breathtaking breadth, depth, and doctrinal density. Several of his recurring themes in particular have commanded my interest since that memorable day twenty-plus years ago. In addition to enhancing my understanding of priesthood and the temple, these sermons have helped me recognize the vital place of women in the Lord's kingdom and increased my appreciation for women's charity and divine nature.

My hope is that a brief review of some of what the Prophet Joseph taught, along with a few reflections, will whet your appetite to study his words in greater detail and depth for yourself. We have been admonished to "seek learning even by study and also by faith."[7] Your insights will be far more relevant and meaningful to you than are mine. My promise is that a study of the Prophet's teachings to women will yield rich spiritual rewards.

The Place of Women in the Kingdom of God

When he set the time and place for the meeting where the Relief Society would be organized, the Prophet Joseph promised the women, "I will organize the women under the priesthood after the pattern of the priesthood."[8] John Taylor, who attended the inaugural meeting with Joseph, declared that the Prophet organized the women "according to the law of Heaven."⁹

After organizing the Relief Society, Joseph stated that "the Church was never perfectly organized until the women were thus organized."¹⁰ He then patterned the new Relief Society presidency like all other presidencies in the Church—after the First Presidency.

That Joseph managed to organize the Relief Society at all was remarkable. These were not carefree days for the Prophet. The year 1842 was not a tranquil time for him. He was contending with an endless parade of threats from his opponents and accusers, ministering to a growing band of beleaguered Saints and immigrants, attempting to build a temple with meager resources, continuing to receive revelations for and in behalf of the Church, and leading a young Church through the intense, step-by-step, line-upon-line process of restoration.

Further, society at large was still highly patriarchal and, as such, strictly limiting of women's rights. Women couldn't vote. (The landmark Seneca Falls Convention, where the push for women's suffrage began in earnest, was still six years away.) Most women were denied higher education, and many weren't formally educated at all. Few had any way of earning money, and if a woman did earn a wage, it legally belonged to her husband. It was still unusual and often difficult for women to own property. And some physical violence against women was not only tolerated socially but protected by law. The bottom line? In 1842, many still viewed women as being just a rung or two higher on the social ladder than prisoners.

So it was in stark contrast to the conventions of the day for the leader of an organization—any organization, let alone the leader of a religion—to give women serious time and attention.

Not only did Joseph organize the Relief Society, attend regularly, and repeatedly teach the women, he often took other Church leaders with him: Brigham Young, John Taylor, Heber C. Kimball, Willard Richards, and George A. Smith, to name a few. It is significant to note that in the first half of the nineteenth century, the Church's presiding leaders found women worth their time.

Simply put, the founding of the Relief Society is evidence of a people who believed in women and their influence and potential. It is the history of an organization destined to provide a framework for women to join together in influence—both in quiet, one-on-one ways and in contributions that affect communities, countries, and even continents for the better. It is the history of an organization destined to elevate women to their proper and appropriate standing. It is a history of vision.

In 1945, Church President George Albert Smith put the organization of the Relief Society into perspective, telling Latter-day Saint women, "You are . . . more blessed than any other women in the world. You were the first women to have the franchise; the first women to have a voice in the work of a church. It was God that gave it to you and it came as a result of revelation to a Prophet of the Lord. Since that time, think what benefits the women of this world have enjoyed. . . . When the Prophet Joseph Smith turned the key for the emancipation of womankind, it was turned for all the world, and from generation to generation the number of women who can enjoy the blessings of religious liberty and civil liberty has been increasing."[11]

Some skeptics have suggested that it took too long (twelve years from the organization of the Church in 1830) to organize the women in 1842. But that perspective is narrow at best. The "restoration of all things" was not simple, formulaic, neat and tidy, or quick.[12] Think of it—the Prophet Joseph was a young adult (just twenty-four years old) when the Church was organized. He had never had a bishop, never been in a quorum, never attended seminary, never had a priesthood leader to nurture him along, never heard a prophet speak. He *was* the prophet. He had no precedent, no manuals, no handbook of instructions. He had to translate the Book of Mormon and then find a way to get it published. All of the revelations expounding doctrine that we turn to so readily and easily in the Doctrine and Covenants were revelations *he* had to receive. And everything he accomplished was against a backdrop of persistent opposition, persecution, and upheaval.

The Restoration took time, line upon line. It was, and is, ongoing.[13] Counselors to Joseph Smith were not even called until 1832, the First Presidency was not organized until a year later, and the Quorum of the Twelve not until 1835. The first endowments were given in 1842, but vicarious endowments for the dead did not commence until January 1877 with the dedication of the St. George Temple. So, despite the centrality to the plan of salvation of sealing generations, it took nearly fifty years from the organization of the Church for all the saving ordinances for the dead to be implemented.[14]

Considering the Saints' constant state of upheaval, the line-upon-line nature of the Restoration, and prevailing societal patriarchy, it is nothing short of incredible that the women were organized at all. If Joseph Smith had been taking his cues from his circumstances or from the world, he most likely wouldn't have bothered. But he was receiving his direction from the Lord.

Elder James E. Talmage declared that "the world's greatest champion of woman and womanhood is Jesus the Christ."[15] The Prophet Joseph was a reflection of the Master he served. He demonstrated by what he said and did that women are vital and integral to building the kingdom of God.[16]

A hundred years later, during the Relief Society centennial year, the First Presidency of the Church would declare, "We ask our Sisters of the Relief Society never to forget that they are a unique organization in the whole world, for they were organized under the inspiration of the Lord. . . . No other woman's organization in all the earth has had such a birth."[17]

Women Are Integral to the Lord's Work

As a young woman in my twenties, I had questions about where women fit in the Lord's Church. Then, in the early 1980s, while I was serving as the Relief Society president in the young adult ward I mentioned earlier, turmoil erupted in the United States surrounding the proposed Equal Rights Amendment, which proponents claimed would erase society's injustices toward women. Responding to revelation, Church leaders opposed the amendment.[18] Sonia Johnson, a member of the Church, campaigned openly against the Church's position, and her advocacy made nationwide news.

Some of the women in my ward, most of whom had to support themselves, were confused about the Church's position.

Others were downright upset. I struggled to understand the issue myself and then to know how to discuss it with women who wondered what could possibly be wrong with legislation that, on the surface, seemed simply to guarantee that they would be paid and treated equally with men.

The spiritual struggle that ensued proved to be a vital learning experience for me. Ironically, it was during that era of upheaval about women in general that I came to feel more peace than I ever had with the roles our Father assigned His daughters. I began to grasp the breadth, distinctions, and magnificence of a righteous woman's influence—and that it comes from a divine endowment that has been in place from the beginning. Though women across the country were inflamed about equal rights, I became absolutely certain that in the only kingdom where it ultimately matters, our Father and His Son uphold women and regard us as central to the plan of salvation.

As Eliza R. Snow, second Relief Society General President, declared in those early days, "We want to be ladies in very deed, not according to the term of the word as the world judges, but fit companions of the Gods and Holy Ones. In an organized capacity we can assist each other in not only doing good but in refining ourselves, and whether few or many come forward and help to prosecute this great work, they will be those that will fill honorable positions in the Kingdom of God."[19]

Through the years, many personal experiences have magnified these truths.

I served as a stake Relief Society president under a stake president who mentored me both by what he said and by what he did. He extended a standing invitation for me to bring anything to his attention that I felt he would want to know. Though I used his invitation carefully, one day I raised a concern about an unproductive pattern I had observed in the working relationships some bishops had with their auxiliary presidents. He responded by inviting me to join him in addressing the subject at an upcoming bishops' training meeting. At the appointed hour, I arrived at the stake center and waited to be invited into the meeting.

When the door opened and I entered the high council room, the stake president quickly rose to his feet, and all the other men followed suit. This gracious, unexpected gesture of respect took my breath away, and a wave of emotion rushed over me. The stake president gestured toward the table where he and his counselors were sitting and said, "Sister Dew, please join us. We have a seat for you with us." He then introduced me by saying, "Brethren, I have invited Sister Dew to discuss a subject *we are both* concerned about. Please listen carefully to what she has to say."

I then delivered the message. When I concluded, the stake president said, "I endorse everything Sister Dew has taught and ask you to act on her suggestions."

Imagine how I felt about serving with a stake president who treated me as a trusted member of his team. I would have walked barefoot on hot coals to help him accomplish the Lord's objectives for our stake.

That experience was literally one of hundreds that demonstrated for me the powerful results of priesthood leaders and auxiliary leaders who unite in purpose and effort. Sister Julie B. Beck, former Relief Society General President, taught that "quorums and Relief Societies are an organized discipleship with the responsibility to assist in our Father's work to bring about eternal life for His children. We are not in the entertainment business; we are in the salvation business. . . . Where quorums and Relief Societies are unified in this work, they each essentially take an oar in the boat—each helping us move toward salvation."[20]

At all levels of Church government, I've had rewarding experiences with priesthood leaders—far too many to count. I have also had bewildering experiences. But does a difficult experience with a priesthood leader mean that priesthood keys and authority aren't real or that there is something inherently wrong with the way the Lord has organized His Church? Of course not. (I hasten to add that I have also had unpleasant experiences with female auxiliary leaders, and I shudder to think about those who have had difficult moments with me.) In a Church of fifteen million members, it is inevitable that even fine leaders—men and women—have days when they don't handle authority very well. Human weakness is a reality in a lay ministry.

Elder Jeffrey R. Holland put it this way: "Be kind regarding human frailty—your own as well as those who serve with you in a Church led by volunteer, mortal men and women. Except in the case of His only perfect Begotten Son, imperfect people are all God has ever had to work with. That must be terribly frustrating to Him, but He deals with it. So should we. And when you see imperfection, remember that the limitation is not in the divinity of the work."[21]

Years ago, Elder Marvin J. Ashton of the Quorum of the Twelve said to me in a moment of private mentoring, "Sheri, don't ever allow yourself to be offended by someone who is learning his job." That is wise counsel.

President Spencer W. Kimball admonished priesthood leaders that "our sisters do not wish to be indulged or to be treated condescendingly; they desire to be respected and revered as our sisters and our equals. I mention [this], my brethren, not because the doctrines or the teachings of the Church regarding women are in any doubt, but because in some situations our behavior is of doubtful quality."[22]

From my experience, most priesthood leaders earnestly seek the help of heaven as they strive to serve the Lord and the people for whom they have responsibility.

When all is said and done, every meaningful opportunity I've ever had to serve and progress has come to me *because* of my membership in the Church. Every single one. And *most* opportunities have been the direct result of a priesthood leader's influence. I have experienced for myself that what the Prophet demonstrated in his interactions with the women of Nauvoo reflects the reality that women hold a vital position in the Church and in the affections of the Lord.

Through the years, I have searched to find *any* organization *anywhere*—any business, charity, religion, or government—where *as many* women have *as much* responsibility and influence as in The Church of Jesus Christ of Latter-day Saints. I cannot find even one. Today millions of Latter-day Saint women in 170-plus countries teach, preach, pray, lead, and preside over auxiliary organizations. And it all began in Nauvoo in 1842 because a Prophet of God organized the women according to the pattern of the Lord.

As an integral part of the Restoration, Joseph Smith restored woman to her rightful place.

Charity and the Divine Nature of Women

Joseph taught the sisters that inherent within their natures were spiritual gifts, beginning with the gift of charity.

Joseph himself was the embodiment of charity. Even as he suffered the hideous incarceration in the Liberty Jail, he admonished his people, "Let thy bowels also be full of charity towards all men, and to the household of faith," promising that if they did, the "doctrine of the priesthood" would distil upon their souls as the dews from heaven.[23]

The Prophet understood that women have a remarkable capacity to understand things of the Spirit and of the heart. As he taught them about their divinely endowed strengths, he added awe-inspiring promises: "The charitable Society—this is according to your natures—it is natural for females to have feelings of charity—you are now plac'd in a situation where you can act according to those sympathies which God has planted in your bosoms. . . .—if you live up to your privileges, the angels cannot be restrain'd from being your associates—females, if they are pure and innocent can come into the presence of God."[24]

This one statement alone is laden with both doctrine and promise: that our Father endowed His daughters with charity; that if we live up to the spiritual privileges of being a woman, angels can't be restrained from watching over and accompanying us;[25] and that purity will lead us into the presence of God.

In a later meeting, Joseph picked up the theme of charity again, explaining its power: "Nothing is so much calculated to lead people to forsake sin as to take them by the hand and watch over them with tenderness. When persons manifest the least kindness and love to me, O what pow'r it has over my mind, while the opposite course has a tendency to harrow up all the harsh feelings and depress the human mind." He continued with a warning and a promise: "tis the doctrine of the devil to retard the human mind and retard our progress, by filling us with self-righteousness—The nearer we get to our heavenly Father, the more are we dispos'd to look with compassion on perishing souls—to take them upon our shoulders and cast their sins behind our back."[26]

No wonder he explained from the beginning that the purpose of Relief Society was to "save souls."[27]

Joseph Smith championed women and womanhood. But he also cautioned women about their innate weaknesses and unrighteous tendencies, including behaviors that threaten charity. In fact, in *every single sermon* to the sisters of Nauvoo, he warned them about their tendency to gossip, backbite, and judge one another, and he took square aim at self-righteousness.

Acknowledging difficulties he had faced because of aspiring men, "great big Elders," as he called them, "who had caused him much trouble" and who had even proclaimed *his* revelations as their own, he warned the women that the "same aspiring disposition will be in this Society, and must be guarded against."[28] Here is just one warning from each sermon:

- "Do not injure the character of any one—if members of the Society shall conduct improperly, deal with them, and keep all your doings within your own bosoms, and hold all characters sacred."[29]

- "All must act in concert or nothing can be done."[30]

- "Don't be limited in your views with regard to your neighbors' virtues, but be limited towards your own virtues, and not think yourselves more righteous than others; you must enlarge your souls toward others if [you would] do like Jesus."[31]

- "Put a double watch over the tongue. . . . The tongue is an unruly member—hold your tongues about things of no moment, a little tale will set the world on fire."[32]

- "We are full of selfishness—the devil flatters us that we are very righteous, while we are feeding on the faults of others."[33]

- "Little evils do the most injury to the church. If you have evil feelings and speak of them to one another, it has a tendency to do mischief."[34]

In cautioning the sisters about their weaknesses, the Prophet was also preparing them for the difficult days ahead, in which unity would be crucial. "By union of feeling we obtain pow'r with God," he taught the sisters.[35]

His words no doubt helped many. Helen Mar Whitney described the power of charity in operation during the exodus from Nauvoo: "The love of God flowed from heart to heart till the wicked one seemed powerless in his efforts to get between us and the Lord, and his cruel darts, in some instances, were shorn of their sting."[36]

What Is the Significance Today of What the Prophet Taught?

Bad girls. Mean girls. Selfish girls. Almost anywhere you look today, there are evidences—and plenty of them—of womanhood gone awry. The Apostle Paul warned that it would come to this. Foreseeing the last days, he described "silly women laden with sins, led away with divers lusts," who would be "ever learning, and never able to come to the knowledge of the truth."[37] And Isaiah foresaw "daughters of Zion" who had become "haughty" and who walked "with stretched-forth necks and wanton eyes, walking and mincing as they go, and making a tinkling with their feet."[38]

Let's face it: Today silly women mired in the sophistries and seductions of the world—and haughty women obsessed with themselves—abound. Regrettably, many women succumb to the temptation to judge, gossip, and undermine one another.

This is nothing if not predictable. Satan will do anything in his considerable power to neutralize the best of our divine nature by exploiting our vulnerabilities. He is expert at turning empathy into envy and charity into criticism. He knows that women filled with pride or jealousy are roadblocks to the Lord's work, and if he can preoccupy us with feelings of inferiority or superiority—he can exploit either—he has a natural inroad to afflict families, friendships, and communities.

And yet, of all women, we ought to be women of charity.

We perhaps underestimate the significance of Joseph's statement that "it is natural for females to have feelings of charity," which are sympathies that "God has planted in [our] bosoms."[39]

Charity is not an emotion or an action. It is not something we feel or do. *Charity is who the Savior is.* It is His most defining and dominant attribute. It is what enabled Him to endure the Garden and the cross for you and me. It is one of the things that makes Him God. Thus, when we plead for the gift of charity, we aren't asking for kind feelings toward someone who has wounded us. We are pleading for our very natures to be changed, for our character to become more and more like the Savior's, so that we literally feel as He would feel and do what He would do. This is why Mormon said that when the Savior appears, those who have been gifted with charity will be like Him, for they will "see him as he is."[40]

The one sure measure of an individual's conversion to Jesus Christ is how that person treats others—in other words, his or her charity. When we turn our hearts to the Lord, and as we increasingly become more like Him, we instinctively open our hearts to others. As one example of many, after Alma the Younger's conversion, his thoughts turned immediately to his people, for he "could not bear that any human soul should perish."[41]

Almost every major scriptural sermon—the Sermon on the Mount, King Benjamin's address, Alma's address at the Waters of Mormon, and a number of others—focuses on the way we treat each other. We are admonished to turn the other cheek, to be reconciled to each other, and to love our enemies and pray for those who despitefully use us.

And yet, we often fall for traps Lucifer has laid to estrange us from one another: gossiping, begrudging each others' successes, and judging one another. The Prophet Joseph's language was unmistakable on this subject: "Sisters of this Society, shall there be strife among you? I will not have it—you must repent and get the love of God. Away with selfrighteousness."[42]

It is simply not for us to judge each other. The Lord has reserved that right for Himself. Only He knows our hearts and understands the varying circumstances of our lives.

If there is anywhere in this world where a woman should feel that she belongs—that she is accepted, needed, valued, and loved—it is in this Church and it is in the Relief Society. True charity never fails because the love of the Savior manifested through us won't fail. President Gordon B. Hinckley both challenged and promised us when he said: "Do you want to be happy? . . . Work to lift and serve His sons and daughters. You will come to know a happiness that you have never known before. . . . Let's get the cankering, selfish attitude out of our lives . . . and stand a little taller . . . in the service of others."[43] And in a theme representative of his life, President Thomas S. Monson has counseled us to look beyond ourselves. "Unless we lose ourselves in service to others, there is little purpose to our own lives," he said. "Those who live only for themselves eventually shrivel up and figuratively lose their lives, while those who lose themselves in service to others grow and flourish—and in effect save their lives."[44]

I have seen charity in action in countless settings and cultures. One experience is a reflection of many others: I was called to serve in a stake Relief Society presidency at age thirty-two, and our presidency bonded quickly as dear friends. Because of my work schedule and their large families that kept them running from dawn until way past dusk, we held presidency meetings on weekdays at 5:30 A.M.

One morning the president raised an issue that for some

reason set me off. I climbed on my own Rameumptom, delivered a speech, and left in a huff. But as I drove away, my heart sank. I couldn't believe I had responded to friends in that way. I was desperate to apologize and counted the hours until I could do so.

Finally evening came. Intent on stopping at each of their homes to apologize, I ran by my house first, only to have the doorbell ring as soon as I walked in the door. There stood my friends, dinner in hand. I'll never forget what they said: "This morning wasn't like you. You must be under a lot of pressure. We thought dinner might make you feel better." I couldn't believe the pureness of their hearts. I cried as I apologized.

Imagine what they could have been saying all day. "That little brat!" They could have whipped themselves into a lather and punished me for days. But they didn't. Instead, they gave me the benefit of the doubt. That day I felt what charity feels like. Charity was not the casserole. It was the gentle way my friends handled my mistake. They reached out to a perishing soul with compassion.

Like our Nauvoo sisters who faced the trek west, we have lives that aren't likely to get any easier. We need each other's strength and compassion. We need to be able to lean on, learn from, and help each other along the path.

President Henry B. Eyring has frequently spoken about the virtue of unity. "You have heard [the] message of unity from me more than once," he acknowledged. "I may well speak of it in the future. I have heard it from every prophet of God in my lifetime. A plea for unity was the last message I remember from President David O. McKay. The Lord's prophets have always called for unity. The need for that gift to be granted to us and the challenge to maintain it will grow greater in the days ahead, in which we will be prepared as a people for our glorious destiny."[45]

Unity is a natural outgrowth of charity. If we live up to our privileges, including the privilege of being women blessed with spiritual gifts from our Father, we need never feel alone—because we'll have angels in heaven and on earth to walk beside us.

One woman who demonstrated, for me, unity and charity at its best was Sister Marjorie Hinckley, the wife of President Gordon B. Hinckley. She reminded us, "Sisters, we are all in this together. We need each other. Oh, how we need each other. . . . We need to lock arms and help build the kingdom so that it will roll forth and fill the whole earth."[46]

Sister Hinckley exemplified, without fanfare or a desire to attract anyone's attention, what happens when faith, hope, and charity come together in a man or woman's life. When we really believe in the Savior, as she did, and believe that He will overrule for our good, that kind of faith naturally creates a feeling of hope and optimism that radiates to all. It enables us to hope not just for a better world somewhere out in the great beyond, but for a much better world here and now.

We can have hope for our lives and for our families' lives. We can have hope to endure and do what we have been called upon to do. With that kind of hope and faith, we inevitably start looking outward instead of inward, thinking of others more than ourselves. And that is when pure charity begins to develop and mature. Perhaps the clearest indication that an endowment of the pure love of Christ is growing within us is when our view increasingly turns outward rather than being so focused on ourselves.

How Can Joseph's Sermons to the Sisters of This Dispensation Help Us?

I end where I began, with questions: Why would Joseph Smith have wanted the women of his day to understand their divine nature and their standing in the Church? And do his words to a small group of Latter-day Saint women 175 years ago matter now?

They have never mattered more. If we understand who we are and what God needs us to do, we place ourselves in an optimal position to fulfill the mission for which we were sent into mortality.

President Gordon B. Hinckley declared that when our Father created woman, it was "the crowning of His glorious work." Said he, "I like to regard Eve as His masterpiece after all that had gone before."[47]

As modern-day daughters of Eve, as inheritors of her majesty and her potential, we have work to do and influence to wield. Precisely because of our unprecedented access to both knowledge and technology, we can help advance the cause of Jesus Christ more than any women have ever been able to help. By the same token, however, we are equally well positioned to frustrate the cause of Christ.

Case in point: We have been encouraged to use technology to reach out, and LDS women have taken to the blogosphere in large numbers. Many blogs are excellent—articulate, engaging, inspiring, and on point doctrinally. Some, however, are filled with a kind of "social gospel" that doesn't always represent either the Church or Latter-day Saint women very well. Most likely

OH, HOW WE NEED EACH OTHER

these writers don't mean any harm; they just don't know what we believe. And so their writings are composed of an unfortunate mixture of the philosophies of women sprinkled with truth. The risk is not just in misrepresenting the Lord's Church but in selling it short.

Reflecting on his time with Joseph Smith, President Heber C. Kimball said that the greatest torment the Prophet Joseph endured "and the greatest mental suffering was because this people would not live up to their privileges. . . . He said sometimes that he felt . . . as though he were pent up in an acorn shell, and all because the people . . . would not prepare themselves to receive the rich treasures of wisdom and knowledge that he had to impart. He could have revealed a great many things to us if we had been ready; but he said there were many things that we could not receive because we lacked that diligence . . . necessary to entitle us to those choice things of the kingdom."[48]

In a similar lament, Nephi wrote that too many would "not search knowledge, nor understand great knowledge, when it is given unto them in plainness, even as plain as word can be."[49]

Joseph Smith's six sermons to women are as plain as word can be. I invite you to study them (available online at josephsmith papers.org/paper-summary/nauvoo-relief-society-minute-book). Cross-reference his teachings with those of living prophets, seers, and revelators. Record your questions and learnings. What expands your understanding? What gives you hope? What prompts you to repent? What evokes charity? What gives you confidence to share what you believe with those not of our faith? Most important, what increases your faith in the Lord Jesus Christ?

In that regard, I can attest that the study suggestions President

Russell M. Nelson has made recently—to accept President Monson's admonition to read the Book of Mormon every day and also to read and study every reference to Jesus Christ in the Topical Guide[50]—will bear rich spiritual fruit. Both of these endeavors put us in a position to learn more fully what we believe and to have the Spirit bear witness of divine truths.

Knowing more enables us to do more and to do better. By the very nature of what he chose to teach women, Joseph Smith established expectations for every woman who would have the privilege of living in this great, culminating dispensation—the one foreseen by prophets since the beginning of time, the dispensation of the fulness of times. *Our* dispensation. And the first expectation is that we learn how to *receive* the truths, the spiritual gifts, and the privileges the Lord has offered His true followers.

Our sisters of Nauvoo helped lay the foundation of a great work. They did it against every kind of prevailing emotional, spiritual, and tangible wind.

Now it is our turn.

It is our chance on the big stage to help bear off the kingdom triumphantly. It wasn't easy for them, and it won't be easy for us. But they did it, and so can we.

President Boyd K. Packer's unqualified endorsement of Relief Society is also an unqualified endorsement of the influence of the women of the Church: "I endorse the Relief Society without hesitation, for I know it to have been organized by inspiration from Almighty God. It has been blessed since its organization. I know that it is a rising, and not a setting, sun. I know that the light and the power that emanates from it will increase, not decrease."[51]

If we are willing to become the women the Prophet Joseph

admonished us to become, women who are true followers of Jesus Christ, the encroaching darkness in the world will actually provide our opportunity. For the women of the world will look to us in increasing numbers and will see in the gospel a better way.

One woman who endured the trek west recorded afterward, "I am grateful I was counted worthy to be a pioneer." I am grateful you and I were counted worthy to come now, when everything is on the line, to be the women privileged to help prepare the world for the return of the Son of God.

We can do it. I know we can.

Notes

1. D&C 135:3.
2. In *Journal of Discourses*, 26 vols. (London: Latter-day Saints' Book Depot, 1856–1886), 23:362. A lengthier version of President Cannon's remarks reads: "He was visited constantly by angels; and the Son of God Himself condescended to come and minister unto him, the Father having also shown Himself unto him; and these various angels, the heads of dispensations, having also ministered unto him. . . . [H]e had vision after vision in order that his mind might be fully saturated with a knowledge of the things of God, and that he might comprehend the great and holy calling that God has bestowed upon him. In this respect he stands unique. There is no man in this dispensation can occupy the station that he, Joseph did, God having reserved him and ordained him for that position, and bestowed upon him the necessary power."
3. Joseph Smith Jr., *History of the Church of Jesus Christ of Latter-day Saints*, 7 vols. (Salt Lake City: The Church of Jesus Christ of Latter-day Saints, 1932–1951), 6:50.
4. *History of the Church*, 5:402.
5. In Conference Report, April 1906, 3–4.
6. *Teachings of Presidents of the Church: Joseph F. Smith* (Salt Lake City: The Church of Jesus Christ of Latter-day Saints,1998), 184.
7. D&C 109:7.

8. Recorded by Sarah M. Kimball in 1882 in her capacity as general secretary of the Relief Society, as quoted in *Daughters in My Kingdom* (Salt Lake City: The Church of Jesus Christ of Latter-day Saints, 2011), 12.

9. *Nauvoo Relief Society Minute Book* (hereafter *Minutes*), March 17, 1842. Available online at http://josephsmithpapers.org/paper-summary/nauvoo -relief-society-minute-book.

10. Sarah M. Kimball, "Auto-biography," *Woman's Exponent*, September 1, 1883, 51. On another occasion, Sarah Kimball recalled the words differently, indicating that Joseph said, "I have desired to organize the Sisters in the order of the Priesthood. I now have the key by which I can do it. The organization of the Church of Christ was never perfect until the women were organized." Recorded by Sarah M. Kimball in 1882 in her capacity as general secretary of the Relief Society, "Relief Society Record, 1880–1892," 29, 30, Church History Library, Historical Department of The Church of Jesus Christ of Latter-day Saints.

11. *Relief Society Magazine*, December 1945, 717.

12. D&C 27:6; 86:10.

13. Many revelations and changes in Church administration and organization illustrate this, including the June 8, 1978, revelation extending the privilege of priesthood ordination to all worthy males, and the relatively recent addition of Churchwide Seventies Quorums.

14. After giving the first endowments, the Prophet turned to Brigham Young and said, "Brother Brigham, this is not arranged perfectly; however we have done the best we could under the circumstances in which we are placed. I wish you to take this matter in hand: organize and systematize all these ceremonies" (L. John Nuttall diary, February 7, 1877; see also *BYU Studies* 19, Winter 1979, 159fn).

15. James E. Talmage, *Jesus the Christ* (Salt Lake City: Deseret Book, 1982), 442.

16. Women have always played central roles in the Savior's Church. About the Relief Society, Eliza R. Snow wrote that "although the name may be of modern date, the institution is of ancient origin. We were told by our martyred prophet that the same organization existed in the Church anciently" ("Female Relief Society," *Deseret News*, April 22, 1868).

17. First Presidency message, July 3, 1942, "To the Presidency, Officers and Members of the Relief Society," in *A Centenary of Relief Society, 1842–1942* (Salt Lake City: Deseret News Press, 1942), 7.

18. See "The Church and the Proposed Equal Rights Amendment," *Ensign*, March 1980.

19. Eliza R. Snow, Address to Lehi Ward Relief Society, October 27, 1869, in *Relief Society Minute Book*, 1868–79, Church History Library, 26–27.

20. Julie B. Beck, "Why Are We Organized into Quorums and Relief Societies?" Brigham Young University Devotional address, January 17, 2012.

21. Jeffrey R. Holland, "Lord, I Believe," *Ensign*, May 2013, 94.

22. Spencer W. Kimball, "Our Sisters in the Church," *Ensign*, November 1979, 49.

23. See D&C 121:45.

24. *Minutes*, April 28, 1842.

25. See D&C 76:66–67; 107:19.

26. *Minutes*, June 9, 1842.

27. *Minutes*, June 9, 1842. President Joseph F. Smith elaborated on the purpose of Relief Society when he stated that the sisters were to "look after the spiritual welfare and salvation of the mothers and daughters of Zion; to see that none is neglected, but that all are guarded against misfortune, calamity, the powers of darkness, and the evils that threaten them in the world" (*Gospel Doctrine* [Salt Lake City: Deseret Book, 1999], 385).

28. *Minutes*, April 28, 1842.

29. *Minutes*, March 17, 1842.

30. *Minutes*, March 30, 1842.

31. *Minutes*, April 28, 1842.

32. *Minutes*, May 26, 1842.

33. *Minutes*, June 9, 1842.

34. *Minutes*, August 31, 1842.

35. *Minutes*, June 9, 1842.

36. Helen Mar Whitney, "Scenes and Incidents at Winter Quarters," *Woman's Exponent*, December 1, 1885, 98.

37. 2 Timothy 3:6–7.

38. 2 Nephi 13:16.

39. *Minutes*, April 28, 1842.

40. Moroni 7:48.

41. Mosiah 28:3.

42. *Minutes*, June 9, 1842.

43. *Teachings of Gordon B. Hinckley* (Salt Lake City: Deseret Book, 1997), 597.

44. Thomas S. Monson, "What Have I Done for Someone Today?" *Ensign*, November 2009, 85.

45. Henry B. Eyring, "Our Hearts Knit as One," *Ensign*, November 2008, 68.

46. *Glimpses into the Life and Heart of Marjorie Pay Hinckley,* ed. Virginia H. Pearce (Salt Lake City: Deseret Book, 1999), 254–55.

47. Gordon B. Hinckley, "Daughters of God," *Ensign*, November 1991, 99.

48. In *Journal of Discourses*, 10:167.

49. 2 Nephi 32:7.

50. Russell M. Nelson, "The Book of Mormon: What Would Your Life Be Like without It," *Ensign*, November 2017, 61; "Drawing the Power of Jesus Christ into Our Lives," *Ensign*, May 2017, 39.

51. Boyd K. Packer, "The Relief Society," *Ensign*, November 1978, 9.